The Maid

The Story of Joan of Arc

L. R. Hitchcock

PELICAN PUBLISHING
2019

Library of Congress Cataloging-in-Publication Data

Names: Hitchcock, LeAnne, author.
Title: The maid : the story of Joan of Arc / LeAnne Hitchcock.
Other titles: Story of Joan of Arc
Description: New Orleans, LA : Pelican Publishing, [2019] | Summary: "The story of Joan of Arc is detailed here in rhyme for young adults. From humble beginnings in Domrémy to her end at the pyre, her tale is told in its entirety." | Audience: Grades 7-8. | Audience: Age 12.
Identifiers: LCCN 2019001028| ISBN 9781455625079 (hardcover : alk. paper) | ISBN 9781455625086 (ebook)
Subjects: LCSH: Joan, of Arc, Saint, 1412-1431—Juvenile literature. | Joan, of Arc, Saint, 1412-1431—Juvenile poetry. | Christian women saints—France—Biography—Juvenile literature. | Christian saints—France—Biography—Juvenile literature. | Women soldiers—France—Biography—Juvenile literature. | Soldiers—France—Biography—Juvenile literature. | France—History—Charles VII, 1422-1461—Juvenile literature.
Classification: LCC DC103.5 .H57 2019 | DDC 944/.026092 [B]—dc23 LC record available at https://lccn.loc.gov/2019001028

Printed in the United States of America
Published by Pelican Publishing
New Orleans, LA
www.pelicanpub.com

To Antoinette—who made me do it

Before this age of modern advances,
When horse and arrow were believed first rate,
A war raged between realms England and France,
British king Henry claimed his rule innate.
So began this story of divine fate.

The people of France abhorred the upstart,
And fought the invader with all their might.
For eighty years, war ripped the land apart,
People and soldiers were worn from the plight,
Hunger and fear became their hosts each night.

There lived in the village of Domrémy
A maid of pious and hardworking nerve.
Her village suffered war's acrimony
Thus fraught, she asked her saints the clash to curb.
Instead, they told her it was time to serve.

Saints Michael and Catherine foretold the deeds,
Of Joan the Maid, who would raise French forces,
Lead armies to victory, then proceed
To crown a true king and shift the war's course
From England's triumph to French reign enforced.

A more faithful child was not to be met,
But such a duty was hard to set forth.
Father and Mother did terribly fret,
Saint's voices or no, Joan's place was home's hearth
Not warring with men on the barraged earth.

Fear could not prosper where saints chose to tap.
But sixteen years old with her fate consigned
Joan started her trip to reshape the map,
By riding to Chinon where Charles did pine,
The Dauphin of France, just king by design.

The Dauphin heard accounts of the bold Maid,
That dared claim her calling bound to his throne.
Famed soldiers revered her, and pacts were made
To join her, in faith, to the battle zone
And fight 'til the English were overthrown.

Charles pondered, and deignèd to meet with Joan.
And planned, with his guests, a deceitful guise;
To prove her foresight just tales being sewn,
He swapped his garments, that royalty prized,
With a man common, made prince by disguise.

Joan saw not costume, but the Dauphin's face,
And told him her needs in practical terms,
She must have troops raised and to battle race.
The guests, amazed, believed Joan's claims were firm,
But Charles, unsure, wanted priests to confirm.

Churchmen gathered and had the girl tested,
Three weeks of prodding affirmed her heart pure.
Thus, so enforced, Charles fully invested,
Fitting the Maid with white armor couture,
Knights were furnished arms, and warhorses sure.

Joan saw a sword in a vision trusted,
Entombed under church altar it did shine
Etched with five crosses, though veiled and rusted,
Once dug from the earth proved metal most fine,
A gift to the Maid, a stout blade divine.

To Orléans her fighters marched with haste.
The town was falling to enemy rule,
Besieged by Burgundians who laid waste
Looting the city in king's name most cruel.
People were starved and despaired from misrule.

The town walls and gates barred the French soldiers,
All entries blockaded with guards entrenched.
Joan gauged the borders and found exposure,
The battle was on and French success clenched.
Orléans was free with mortal needs quenched.

JHESUS
MARIA

For Patay city, Joan next plied her shield.
The fighting so fierce it silenced brave hearts,
Victory's tithe paid by wounds never healed.
Weeping for tarnished souls lost to war's arts,
Joan prayed for felled friends and foes departed.

A woman of action was the good Maid.
She rode to Reims with the prince to advance
The saint's instructions to have a king made.
At last, Charles was crowned the monarch of France,
Bonding the power of the resistance.

The crown finally placed righteous and true,
Charles toured his states, sensing love all around.
He gathered support to hold a short truce,
Planning as king, English claims to breakdown.
This gave the enemy time to rebound.

City of Paris, bright jewel in the crown,
Was held by the English causing dismay.
The truce over, Joan's troops raided the town,
But the foe was rested and quick to fray,
They vanquished the poor Maid and won the day.

The Paris defeat unmasked fickle souls,
Who taxed Joan's name and besmirched her until
Charles came to suppose she upset his goals.
But strong and loyal were some soldiers still,
Three hundred valiant men marched to her will.

JHESUS MARIA

On to Compiègne her small force did turn,
An English duke claimed the right to dictate
The people and lands his breed did not earn.
He'd taken command of the city's gates,
But the town rebelled and for Joan did wait.

With her arrival the companies clashed,
But, being outstripped Joan's soldiers were slain.
She called for retreat and left the field last,
To ensure her men gained safety again.
Her flag held high though she'd lost the campaign.

An English born archer loathed the brash Maid.
Though she withdrew, he assaulted her horse
And yanked Joan's gold vest 'til aground she laid,
Then commenced in swordplay expert and coarse.
Thus, trapping the girl by use of grim force.

At time of her seizure, fair trade in use
Was to pay cash for a captive's release.
Charles, planning to wager a prolonged truce,
Would risk no ransom to prevent the peace.
He left Joan to fate and his foe's caprice.

Ten thousand gold livres the English paid
To have Joan conveyed to Rouen for trial.
As soldier of war no plots were forbade,
Still, the British cast her godless and vile
And locked her in chains and quarters hostile.

Bishop Pierre Cauchon ran the events,
Where the church sat as judge, not worldly law.
Denied lawyers to act in her defense,
Joan stood to be tried without charges drawn,
The court inclined to make her England's pawn.

Cauchon did search for reason to convict,
But the Maid's honor proved hard to impeach.
When provoking her with words of conflict,
Joan's chaste convictions kept charge of her speech,
And she stung the men who claimed finer reach.

The bench failed to refute Joan's moral facts
Or prove her council demonic factions.
The clothes she wore and her soldiering acts
Became the focus of judges' sanctions,
Marked as grave sins in need of retractions.

The clergy presented Joan a sworn writ.
She would be allowed Mass and to walk free,
By shunning male dress and armed feats forfeit.
Ill from remand, though prone to disagree,
She longed for pardon and signed the decree.

will in future
neither carry arms,
nor wear men's clothes
nor cut my hair short.
Jehanne

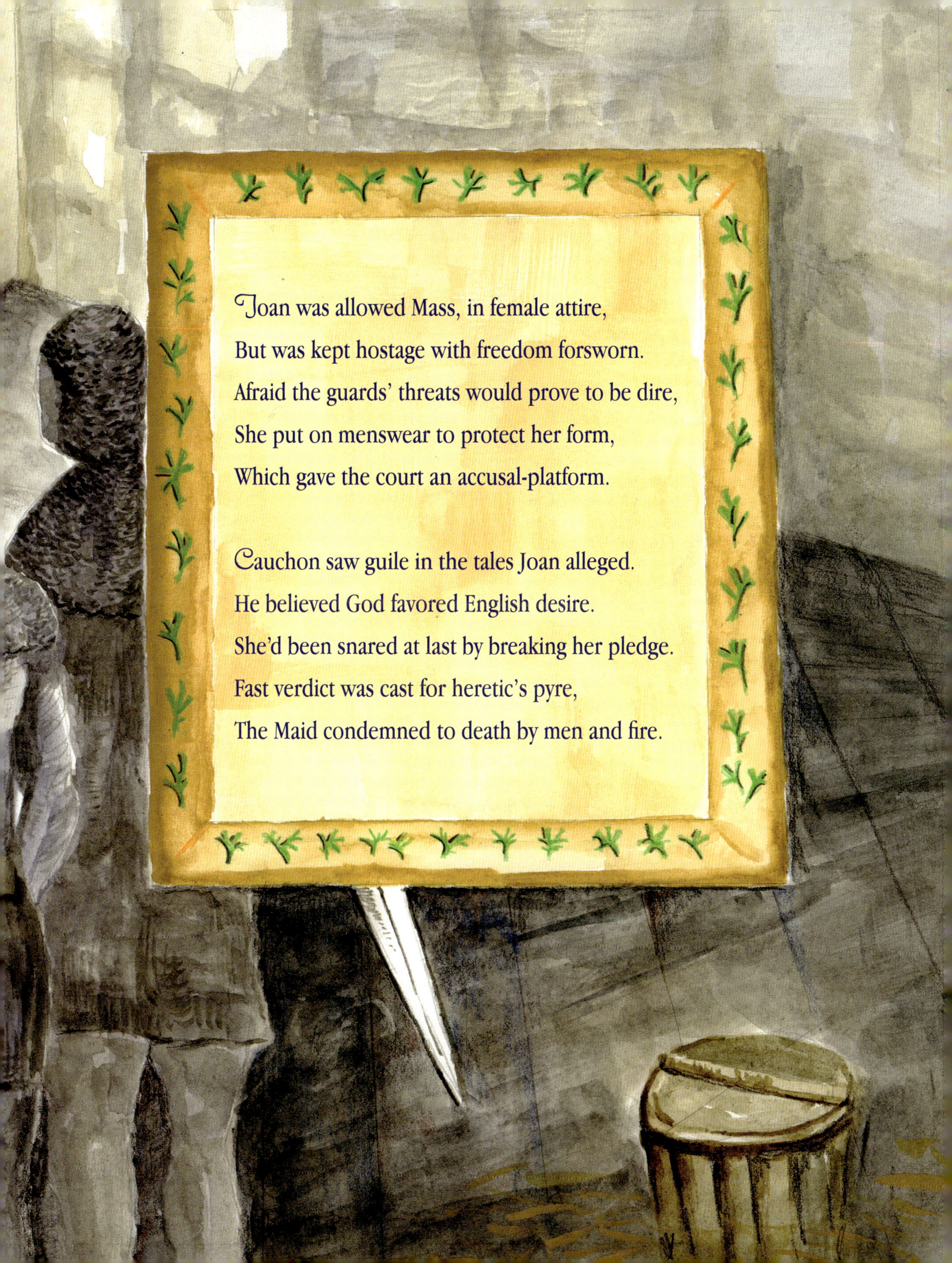

Joan was allowed Mass, in female attire,
But was kept hostage with freedom forsworn.
Afraid the guards' threats would prove to be dire,
She put on menswear to protect her form,
Which gave the court an accusal-platform.

Cauchon saw guile in the tales Joan alleged.
He believed God favored English desire.
She'd been snared at last by breaking her pledge.
Fast verdict was cast for heretic's pyre,
The Maid condemned to death by men and fire.

Joan bravely endured the pain, fire, and smoke,
Calling out to Jesus in bright refrains,
That shamed her captors 'til guilty tears broke.
The Maid remained faithful and one guard claims,
A white dove did fly direct from the flames.

A witness of note knew Joan as a girl
And followed her trial with honest concern.
She saw the killing and watched the blaze curl,
Though lighted three times, the flames were all spurned.
She swore to her death Joan's heart would not burn.

Twenty years on, the French kingdom was free.
Charles, triumphant, sought Joan's honor to clear,
And called a review of her death decree.
Her judges and guards were named to appear,
But some stayed hidden due to cowards' fear.

Witnesses came forward with tales profound,
Causing Joan's staunch valor to be retraced.
It was hailed her harsh punishments unfound,
And her name was returned to holy grace.
At last the Maid awarded hero's place.

US MARIA

Joan's story was told for hundreds of years,
'til the Church named her a maiden extolled.
As Saint Joan of Arc, she joined her blessed peers,
By urging the prayerful to be consoled,
Whispering courage and faith to uphold.

The Maid is still treasured the world around,
Parades are held to act out her choices.
From Orléans, France, to New Orleans town,
Praise is paid to the girl, who heard voices,
With her flag raised and singing rejoices.

And so it was writ, and that is the truth.

"One life is all we have; we live it as we believe."
-Joan of Arc-
"I am not afraid, I was born to do this."
-Joan of Arc-
"Act, and God will act."
-Joan of Arc-
léans

Author's note

Joan's courage, faith, and refusal to give in to social norms have made her an inspiration for centuries.

Joan's story has been told many times, and in many ways. I chose to tell her story in iambic pentameter because the poetic form ensured that each word and phrase moved the story forward in a concise way. The first appearance of the style is up for debate, but it is probably most recognized in the works of Shakespeare, which were created over a hundred years after Joan's death.

The illustrations reference the colorful paintings and manuscripts of the Middle Ages, which placed an emphasis on biblical stories and symbolism, including the allegorical meanings of plants and animals. The bay leaf, for example, represents purity, while violets symbolize loyalty. In this book, various flowers and herbs border the text to accent points of the story. Animals are used in the same way. The image of three crows flying over Joan and her family before her departure are ill omens.

The life of Joan of Arc was controversial in her day, and remains so for modern readers. Her trial was well documented, with transcripts recorded in French, English, and Latin, making the truth of their content difficult to dispute. The questions surrounding Joan are ones of faith. Did she really have a vision of a sword under a church altar, or had she been given more earthly knowledge of its burial? Did she receive instructions from the saints, or did she suffer from delusions? These are questions that can only be answered based on individual beliefs. It is partly because of these unanswerable factors that Joan remains a figure of admiration and mystery. Uncertainties aside, Joan of Arc will always be the teenager who helped crown a king and turn the tide of the Hundred Years' War in France's favor.

A brief timeline of events in Joan's life:

Jan. 6, 1412	Joan is born.
Feb. 13, 1429	Joan travels to Chinon, wearing men's clothing, to meet with Charles the Dauphin.
April 1429	Charles provides Joan with a small army.
April 29 - May 4, 1429	The Battle of Orléans is fought and Joan is victorious.
June 18, 1429	The Battle of Patay, where Joan wins the day.
July 17, 1429	Charles is crowned king in the city of Reims. Joan is in attendance holding her standard, to the disapproval of some.
May 1430	Joan is captured after losing the Battle of Compiègne.
Jan. 13, 1431	Joan's trial begins.
May 29, 1431	Joan is convicted of heresy and handed over to a secular court.
May 30, 1431	Joan is executed by burning at the stake.
1450	Charles VII orders an investigation of Joan's trial resulting in all charges being cleared.
May 16, 1920	Pope Benedict XV makes Joan a saint.